Original title:
The Frozen Solstice



Author: Kätriin Kaldaru
ISBN HARDBACK: 978-9908-1-1750-8
ISBN PAPERBACK: 978-9908-1-1751-5
ISBN EBOOK: 978-9908-1-1752-2

## Frost-strewn Tales beneath a Shimmering Sky

Beneath the stars, we gather near,
Laughter dances, smiles sincere.
The cold air sparkles, a wintry delight,
Stories unfold in the soft, still night.

The moon casts pearls on the icy ground,
As joy and warmth in our hearts abound.
We toast to dreams with cups held high,
Under the watch of a shimmering sky.

Snowflakes twirl, like whispers of cheer,
In this festive moment, all draw near.
With every glance, the magic we weave,
In frost-strewn tales, we truly believe.

Join hands together, feel the embrace,
Of winter's charm, a timeless grace.
In this wonder, we find our bliss,
Beneath the stars, none shall miss.

## Celestial Harmony in Frost

Winter's breath paints the world so bright,
Each flake a note in the silent night.
Harmony whispers in the chill of the air,
As laughter and joy fill the frosty square.

Under the glow of the twilight's muse,
Voices join in a festive blues.
Bells ringing softly, a melody clear,
Resonating warmth filled with cheer.

Children's giggles, a sweet serenade,
As snowballs fly like a playful cascade.
Together we shine in the cold's warm embrace,
A celestial harmony, love interlaced.

So let us dance in this winter trance,
Spinning and twirling, we seize every chance.
In the heart of frost, we find our light,
As the world sparkles with pure delight.

## Dreaming Beneath the Winter Stars

In the stillness of night, dreams take flight,
Beneath a blanket of stars, oh so bright.
The frost-kissed ground whispers tales untold,
Of magic and wonder, a vision to hold.

Candles flicker, illuminating smiles,
As we gather together across the miles.
With cocoa warm and spirits high,
We find our joy in the winter sky.

Every twinkle, a promise we make,
In the heart of the cold, our souls awake.
With every heartbeat, old stories revive,
Under the glow, we feel so alive.

The night wraps around us, a velvet embrace,
In dreams of winter, we find our place.
So raise a glass to the stars above,
In this festive moment, we feel the love.

## An Offering to Winter's Embrace

Gather around, for the season is here,
An offering to winter, a time to draw near.
With laughter like music, and hearts that ignite,
We welcome the magic that sparkles tonight.

The fire crackles, its warmth our delight,
As stories of old dance in the light.
We hang up our wishes, on branches of pine,
In winter's embrace, our spirits align.

Chill in the air, but our hearts feel so bold,
In the season of giving, let the warmth unfold.
With cookies and cocoa, we savor the taste,
In the glow of the moment, no time to waste.

Winter's enchantment whispers so sweet,
As friends and loved ones gather to meet.
In this festive embrace, we find our way,
With love as our guide, we cherish the day.

## Harmonies of Solstice Stillness

Under twinkling stars bright, a choir sings,
Warm hearts aglow, as the season brings.
Joyful laughter fills the chilled night air,
Hands held together, love beyond compare.

Candles flicker softly, shadows dance bold,
Stories exchanged, as the night unfolds.
Mirthful spirits sway, in a gentle embrace,
Memories woven, time won't erase.

## A Quiet Journey through Winter Trails

Snowflakes whisper secrets, a soft, white hush,
Footsteps crunch lightly, in the quiet rush.
Frosted branches shimmer, in the pale moon's glow,
Each breath is a marvel, in the fresh, crisp snow.

A wooden sleigh glides, down the hill with glee,
Children's joyful shouts, wrapping laughter free.
Hot cocoa warms fingers, as the night draws near,
Cozy gatherings spark, a bond sincere.

## Dance of Frosted Leaves in the Wind

Leaves twirl and flutter, in a frosty ballet,
Nature's festive whispers, lead the joyful play.
Branches sway gently, to the crisp, cool air,
Mirrored in the laughter, as spirits declare.

Glistening pathways call, under a moonbeam's glow,
Every step a promise, of warmth and friendly show.
Circles of friends gather, in a joyful embrace,
Cherishing moments, in this magical space.

## Secrets Entwined in Winter's Grasp

Veils of white blanket secrets, softly they sleep,
In the heart of winter, dreams begin to creep.
Branches hug tightly, under the moon's glance,
Whispers of hope flutter, in a snowy dance.

The warmth of togetherness, ignites the cold night,
With stories of old, we find pure delight.
Burning firelight glimmers, in the still twilight,
Hearts drawing closer, under the starry sight.

## Frosted Echoes of Timelessness

Snowflakes dance in joyous flight,
Laughter rings through the chilly night.
Candles flicker, warm and bright,
Hearts embrace the pure delight.

Whispers soft as winter's breath,
Celebrating life and death.
Time stands still, a moment's grace,
In this enchanted, frosted space.

A tune of joy floats on the air,
As friends unite with love to share.
The world in white, a canvas grand,
Together we will make our stand.

Frosted echoes linger long,
In every heart we sing our song.
Memories dance like stars above,
Embraced in warmth and endless love.

## A Twilight Mantle of White

Twilight falls on a snowy scene,
Blankets of white, where we have been.
Under blankets, dreams take flight,
Wrapped in joy, all feels so right.

Hot cocoa warms our chilly hands,
We carve our names in snowy lands.
A fireplace glows, the shadows play,
In winter’s hug, we wish to stay.

Stars twinkle bright in velvet skies,
As laughter brings forth shining eyes.
Every moment a treasure, fine,
With friends and family, hearts align.

The night unfolds with purest bliss,
Each frosted breath, a dreamy kiss.
Beneath the mantle of twilight white,
We celebrate this magic night.

## Silence Beneath the Stars

Silence wraps the world in peace,
Under starlit skies, joy won't cease.
Frosted whispers fill the air,
A hush of wonder, everywhere.

Snowflakes fall with gentle grace,
Painting love on every face.
Chill of night, yet hearts are warm,
In this stillness, we find our charm.

Friends gather close, beneath the glow,
In this moment, time moves slow.
With open arms, we grasp the night,
A tapestry of hearts alight.

Every twinkle tells a tale,
Of laughter shared and love set sail.
In silence deep, our souls align,
Beneath the stars, our joys entwine.

## Frosted Branches, Silent Wishes

Frosted branches reach for sky,
In their beauty, dreams float by.
With every wish upon the breeze,
A silent prayer among the trees.

Nighttime whispers, soft and clear,
Echoing in the hearts so dear.
Footprints trace our joyful dance,
In this magic, we take a chance.

Together, we sing the night along,
With laughter, light, and vibrant song.
Hope ignites like stars out bright,
As we embrace this wondrous sight.

Frosted wonders, wishes shared,
A bond of love, forever cared.
In every branch, our hopes are found,
Within this joy, our hearts unbound.

## Awakened Dreams of a Crystal Realm

In the heart of night, stars gleam bright,
Whispers of joy take their flight,
Crystals dance in the moon's embrace,
Dreams awaken in this magical space.

Laughter echoes through the trees,
Carried by a gentle breeze,
Sparkling lights, a festive show,
In the realm where the wonders flow.

Hope ignites in every heart,
Creating bonds that never part,
With each twirl, the world spins free,
Awakened dreams, in harmony.

Together we weave a tale so grand,
In this crystal realm, we stand,
With souls alight, we join the scheme,
Chasing the magic of a shared dream.

## Dance of Shadows in Winter Light

Frosted branches, a winter's song,
The dance of shadows, all night long,
In the glow of lanterns, spirits rise,
Through the darkness, under starlit skies.

Snowflakes drift on the whispering air,
Each unique, with a tale to share,
As laughter twirls in the chilly night,
We find warmth in the festive light.

Footprints trace a joyful path,
In the glow of laughter, feel the warmth bath,
With every heartbeat, spirits blend,
In the dance of shadows, friendships mend.

Around the fire, stories unfold,
Of winter nights and dreams retold,
In this moment, we are alight,
As we embrace the winter's light.

**Celestial Snowfall and Quiet Resolutions**

Under the gaze of a silver moon,
Softly falls the winter's tune,
Each flake a promise, pure and bright,
In the stillness, we grasp delight.

Families gather, hearts entwined,
With whispered wishes, hope aligned,
The air is filled with gentle cheer,
In the quiet, the new year draws near.

Candles flicker, casting dreams,
In their glow, a future gleams,
With every sigh, we release the past,
Embracing the joy that will last.

Around the table, laughter flows,
In the warmth, a love that grows,
Celestial dreams, radiant and real,
In this moment, our hearts reveal.

## Untold Stories of Winter's Embrace

In the hush of night, stories arise,
Wrapped in the warmth of starry skies,
Footsteps in snow, the echoes of cheer,
Each moment whispers tales, sincere.

Wrapped in layers, we gather tight,
In winter's embrace, hearts feel light,
Candles flicker, shadows sway,
As we share the love of the day.

Laughter dances, a sweet refrain,
In this season, there's no room for pain,
Hugs like blankets, cozy and warm,
Embracing each other, we feel the charm.

Together we share the old and new,
With festive hearts, we chart the hue,
In winter's embrace, we find our song,
Untold stories where we all belong.

**Frozen Rainbows on the Horizon**

Colors blend from sky to ground,
A canvas bright, the joy we found.
Each droplet shines like tiny gems,
As laughter dances, joy transcends.

Children play in shimmering light,
Chasing dreams, hearts taking flight.
In every splash and every cheer,
The warmth of love draws us near.

Nature's art, a wondrous feast,
Celebration, to say the least.
With friends and family all around,
Frozen rainbows in joy abound.

## Serenity in a Snow-Covered World

Blankets white on every lane,
Soft and sweet as whispered rain.
The world transformed to stillness pure,
In winter's grasp, our hearts secure.

Footprints dance where silence lay,
Magic twirls in bright array.
Hot cocoa warms our chilly hands,
As joy unfolds in gentle strands.

Under stars, the night aglow,
Heartfelt tales in soft winds blow.
With every snowflake, dreams take flight,
Serenity wraps us, oh so tight.

## A Silhouette in Winter's Glow

In twilight's hush, the shadows grow,
A figure moves through soft, white snow.
With every step, a story weaves,
Of secrets held and hopes that cleave.

The warmth of laughter lingers near,
In twinkling lights, we shed our fear.
A silhouette, bold and free,
In winter's glow, we dare to be.

Together we dance, hearts in tune,
Beneath the soft embrace of moon.
Every moment, a spark ignites,
In winter's breath, our spirit lights.

## Wreaths of Frost in a Moonlit Glade

In glades adorned with silver lace,
Frosted wreaths, a hidden place.
The air smells sweet with pine and cheer,
As winter whispers, calm and clear.

Moonlight shimmers on icy dreams,
Casting spells with silver beams.
Gathered friends share tales so bright,
In nature's arms, by firelight.

Around us, wonder starts to bloom,
As laughter banishes the gloom.
In this glade, where hearts align,
Wreaths of frost, our love will shine.

## Glacial Mirrors of the Soul

In the twilight's gentle glow,
Reflections dance on ice so slow.
Wonders twinkle, hearts align,
A vibrant pulse in frosty brine.

Laughter echoes through the night,
While stars above shine pure and bright.
We raise our cups to cheer and sing,
Embracing joy that winter brings.

Whispers of the past take flight,
As snowflakes swirl in pure delight.
Each glacial shard a story told,
In sparkling hues of blue and gold.

Together we weave a tapestry,
Of frosty dreams and harmony.
In this moment our spirits soar,
In glacial mirrors, we explore.

## Lullaby of the Snowflakes

Softly falls the winter's grace,
Snowflakes twirl in their embrace.
A lullaby, they gently sing,
As whispers of the season ring.

In dreamy realms where shadows play,
The world adorned in white display.
Each flake a note in nature’s song,
A symphony where we belong.

Underneath the moon’s soft light,
Children laugh, hearts warm and bright.
With every flurry, joy’s rebirth,
A lullaby of peace on earth.

So let us dance in pure delight,
As snowflakes join our festive night.
In this magic, we are whole,
Embracing love, the heart and soul.

## Shards of Light in the Abyss

Amidst the cold, where shadows creep,
Shards of light through darkness leap.
A fiery glow breaks winter's chill,
With hope and warmth, the heart will fill.

Candles flicker in soft embrace,
Glowing bright in this boundless space.
Each spark ignites a fervent dream,
In the abyss, we brightly gleam.

Voices rise like music sweet,
Rhythms dance upon our feet.
Together in this vibrant glow,
In festive jubilance, we grow.

Shards of light, a tapestry,
Woven through our memory.
In shadows dark, we find our way,
Guided by the light of day.

## Portrait of a Wintry Reverie

On canvas white, the stories freeze,
A portrait painted by the breeze.
With every stroke, a memory bright,
A wintry reverie ignites the night.

Hoarfrost whispers on the trees,
Nature's art, a masterpiece.
In swirling winds, two hearts entwine,
With joy and laughter intertwined.

Sipping cocoa by the fire,
As dreams alight, they lift us higher.
Each moment wrapped in purest lace,
In wintry wonder, we find our place.

So here we stand, and here we stay,
In this portrait, come what may.
With festive spirits, we embrace,
The beauty of this sacred space.

## The Stillness of Frost-Kissed Mornings

The sun peeks softly, golden light,
Frosted whispers greet the day,
Laughter dances in the air,
Joyful hearts come out to play.

Snowflakes shimmer, twirling bright,
Children's smiles, dreams take flight,
Warm mugs clink, friendships toast,
In this magic, we can boast.

The world aglow, a canvas white,
Footprints trace our paths so bright,
Nature holds her breath in glee,
A festive moment, wild and free.

As bells ring out, the spirits rise,
In frost-kissed mornings, love never dies,
We gather close, our voices cheer,
Eternal memories, held so dear.

## Ethereal Glimmers in Twilight

As daylight fades, the stars awake,
Soft hues dance on the silent lake,
Whispers of night begin to sing,
The festive magic that twilight brings.

With lanterns glimmering in the breeze,
We gather under the shimmering trees,
Stories shared with laughter's embrace,
In every heart, a warm, bright space.

The moon takes charge, its silver glow,
Filling the night with a radiant show,
Cheerful voices blend and soar,
Creating memories we all adore.

In this twilight, we're never apart,
A festival of joy, a work of art,
Hand in hand, through shadows we roam,
In ethereal glimmers, we find our home.

## Gathering Frosted Memories

In the chill of a winter's eve,
We come together, hearts believe,
Frosted branches, crystal dreams,
Endless laughter, soft moonbeams.

Trimming trees, a festive sight,
With every laugh, the world feels right,
Songs of joy fill the frosty air,
In this gathering, love lays bare.

Bundled tight in scarfs and mittens,
Sharing tales that brighten fittin's,
Cookies baked, the scents divine,
In frosted memories, we intertwine.

With every cheer, our spirits lift,
This season's magic is the greatest gift,
Around the fire, the stories flow,
Gathering warmth in the winter's glow.

## Where the Nights Hang Heavy

Where the nights hang heavy with cheer,
The world adorned in festive gear,
Laughter echoes through the dark,
A special glow from every spark.

Hot cocoa flows, the fire bright,
Families gather, hearts alight,
Twinkling lights, a wondrous sight,
In this embrace, we share the night.

Harmonies rise, a joyful tune,
Beneath the watchful, silver moon,
Whispers of hope fill the air,
Together we find love everywhere.

As stories weave through the cold,
In every heart, a warmth unfolds,
Nights hang heavy, but joy won't cease,
In this spirit, we find our peace.

## Chilling Serenade of Shadows

In the quiet night, the stars gleam,
Whispers of joy in the frosty dream.
Snowflakes dance, a whimsical flight,
Carols echo, hearts feel light.

Laughter drifts on the icy breeze,
Gather 'round, let worries freeze.
A tale unfolds by the fire's glow,
Under soft blankets, we feel the flow.

Merry faces, old friends reunite,
Warmth surrounds us, hearts ignite.
In this moment, let time suspend,
A chilling serenade, sweet joy we send.

As shadows play in the candle's light,
We celebrate the enchanting night.
Together we share this festive cheer,
A melody of love, we hold dear.

## The Long Wait for Warmth to Return

Snow blankets all in a quilted white,
Winter’s grip holds the world so tight.
Yet in our hearts, a flicker remains,
Hope for sunshine after the rains.

Gathered round, with cocoa so warm,
We weave our dreams, in quiet charm.
Fires crackle, while stories unfold,
Serenades sung in whispers bold.

The days grow long, the chill begins to wane,
A promise made, we'll feel the gain.
Laughter resounds as blossoms bloom,
Spring's sweet kiss will erase the gloom.

Through frosty nights, we shall delight,
In the long wait for warmth's sweet invite.
Each star above twinkles like a friend,
Together, we cheer, for soon it will end.

## Beneath the Icebound Gaze

Underneath the moon's soft light,
The world lies still, in blanket white.
Glistening crystals, a magical sight,
Invite us to revel in this beautiful night.

Whispers of winter dance in the air,
Each flake a promise, delightful and rare.
A joyful spirit, a festive cause,
We celebrate nature's perfect pause.

Friends gather close, with smiles so bright,
Stories shared, hearts feel light.
In harmony, we greet the chill,
Finding warmth in laughter, a timeless thrill.

With every sip from a steaming mug,
We wrap ourselves in joy, snug as a bug.
Beneath the icebound gaze we stand,
Together as one, hand in hand.

## Shadows of Winter's Whisper

Softly the snow falls, a gentle sigh,
Winter's shadow dances in the night sky.
Crisp air carries tales of old,
A tapestry of memories, woven in gold.

The flickering flames bring life and cheer,
Each laugh, each smile, echoes near.
In this embrace of frost and flame,
We kindle the spirit, we play the game.

Carols rise like a sweet serenade,
Together we gather, no fear of fade.
Shadows of winter painted anew,
With warmth of friendship, forever true.

So let the snow blanket the ground,
In this festive night, love is found.
With every heartbeat, under the stars,
We create our joy, no matter how far.

## Glimmering Pathways through Winter's Woods

Beneath the frosted boughs we tread,
A glimmering path where dreams are spread.
Twinkling lights dance in the trees,
Whispers of joy in the crisp winter breeze.

Laughter echoes, vibrant and bright,
As stars above twinkle with delight.
Footprints crunched in the glistening snow,
Guiding us onward where cheer does grow.

Hot cocoa warms our chilly hands,
Stories unfold as the evening stands.
Together we share in this festive cheer,
In winter's embrace, love draws us near.

As snowflakes fall, a soft serenade,
Creating a wonderland where joy won't fade.
With hearts aglow and laughter alight,
We celebrate life on this magical night.

## Echoes of Forgotten Hues

In twilight's glow, colors collide,
Echoes of hues where dreams abide.
Pastel skies of orange and blue,
Paint the memories that once flew.

Lively sounds fill the frosty air,
The carolers' songs awaken a flare.
With every note, the past is revived,
In joyous moments, our spirits derived.

Sparkling lanterns guide the way,
As darkness fades, brightens the day.
Children dance beneath the stars,
Woven together, forgetting the scars.

This festive night unfolds like a scroll,
Intwined in laughter, it nourishes the soul.
With every heartbeat, memories weave,
In echoes of hues, we learn to believe.

## Portrait of a Winter Wonderland

A canvas of white, pure and bright,
Crafting a portrait in soft, fading light.
Pine trees draped in a frosty shawl,
Dancing shadows on the snow-covered hall.

Children's laughter rings in the air,
Snowflakes spinning, a magical affair.
Sleds racing down hills, cheeks aglow,
In this winter wonderland, our spirits flow.

Huddled in circles, friends share a tale,
Warmth in their hearts, on the brisk winter trail.
Candles glimmer, illuminating the night,
Creating a scene, oh, such sheer delight!

With every step taken, joy cascades,
Building snowmen in festive parades.
This portrait we paint with love and glee,
A winter wonderland, forever we'll be.

## Frosty Kisses upon the Earth

Frosty kisses touch the ground,
A whispering chill, a magic found.
Nature’s blanket, soft and white,
Covers the world in pure delight.

Carols sung by the fireside glow,
Embers dancing, hearts in tow.
The scent of pine and spices blend,
A festive warmth that will not end.

Icicles glisten like crystals bright,
Reflecting the stars in the deep night.
Gliding through dreams on this wondrous crest,
In frosty embraces, we feel truly blessed.

With hands held tight, we venture forth,
In winter's chill, we find our worth.
Frosty kisses, our souls ignite,
In joyous gatherings, our spirits take flight.

## Chronicles of a Frozen Twilight

Underneath the starry glow,
Snowflakes dance in joyous flight,
Laughter echoes, hearts aglow,
In the warmth of frozen twilight.

Children twirl in coats of bright,
Chasing dreams on winter's eve,
Glistening pathways filled with light,
Magic weaves what we believe.

Fires crackle, stories shared,
Hot cocoa warms the chilly night,
Together, every heart is bared,
In the glow of festive light.

Memories etched in icy air,
Friendships bloom in shimmering white,
As we gather, free of care,
Chronicles of a frozen night.

## Whispers of Time in White

Whispers float, the night is white,
Silvery trails of moonbeam's dance,
Wrapped in warmth, we feel the height,
Of joyous hearts and spirits' prance.

Icicles glisten, nature's art,
Silent echoes of the past,
As laughter ignites every heart,
Moments treasured, unsurpassed.

Each breath a cloud, horizons wide,
Time stands still in the snowy sea,
With every step, our hopes abide,
This festive night, for you and me.

Through falling flakes, dreams take flight,
Binding souls in soft delight,
Whispers blend with starlit sight,
In unity, we hold the night.

## Crystal Enchantment after Dark

Under the glow of lantern's cheer,
Crystal frost adorns each tree,
Soft enchantments draw us near,
In a world of magic, wild and free.

Frosted wreaths and garlands bright,
Dance in rhythm with the night,
Voices lifted, spirits soar,
In this festive realm, we explore.

Candles flicker, shadows play,
Hearts entwined in joyous throng,
Every glance, a bright bouquet,
In this symphony, we belong.

Crystals sparkle, dreams ignite,
As stars adorn the chilly sky,
By the fire’s warmth, pure delight,
Together with loved ones, we sigh.

## Fragments of Light in a Darkened Glade

In the glade where shadows creep,
Fragments of light begin to bloom,
Festive whispers from the deep,
Guide our hearts to lift the gloom.

Twilight dances, moonlight weaves,
Every branch a story shared,
Nature's canvas softly leaves,
Patterns bright, lovingly prepared.

Underneath the starlit gaze,
Each moment sparkles, crisp and clear,
In the joy of shared displays,
We find warmth, releasing fear.

With laughter ringing, spirits high,
In this haven, love's embrace,
Fragments of light as we vie,
To keep the festive dreams in place.

## Frosted Petals on a Frozen Stream

Frosted petals dance with delight,
Sparkling under the moon's soft light.
Joyful laughter fills the cold air,
Whispers of magic swirling everywhere.

Children in scarves, their cheeks aglow,
Chasing the shadows, letting joy flow.
Laughter erupts like bells in the night,
Hearts entwined in this winter's light.

Branches adorned with shimmering ice,
A wonderland painted, oh so nice.
Every breath forms a glistening plume,
Nature awakes from the chill of gloom.

As stars twinkle bright in the starry dome,
We gather together, we'll make this our home.
Frosted petals on a frozen stream,
In this festive moment, all hearts can dream.

## Secrets of the Midnight Frost

Under the veil of a starry night,
Secrets unfold in delicate light.
Each crystal flake a story to share,
Whispers of wonder fill the brisk air.

The world transforms with a magical embrace,
Frost-kissed petals in a sparkly lace.
Every corner shines with dreams anew,
A canvas of joy in every hue.

Candles aglow 'neath the silver sky,
Laughter and cheer as the moments fly.
Frosty breath mingles in joyous song,
Together we dance, where hearts belong.

As midnight chimes with a festive cheer,
We treasure each moment, loved ones near.
Secrets of frost on this wondrous night,
In the warmth of our hearts, everything feels right.

## A Symphony of Snowflakes

Snowflakes twirl like dancers in flight,
Painting the world in pure, soft white.
Each a note in a symphonic score,
Harmony echoes, we long for more.

Under the moon, we gather and sway,
To the rhythm of winter, brightening the day.
Every swirl brings a festive glee,
In this snowfall choir, we feel so free.

Laughter erupts with each flake that falls,
A melody calling from frosty walls.
Together we sing through the chilly air,
A celebration of warmth, of love to share.

As snow blankets the earth, soft and pure,
We create memories that will endure.
A symphony of snowflakes, wild and bright,
In the heart of winter, everything feels right.

**Ethereal Hues of Night's Canvas**

Ethereal hues dance on the dark,
A canvas of dreams, each twinkling spark.
Colors collide in the frosty night,
Creating a world that feels just right.

Stars whisper softly, secrets arrayed,
In the tapestry of joy we've made.
Underneath this shimmering dome,
We find our hearts in a festive home.

Joyful are the moments shared anew,
Binding us closer, like morning dew.
With every heartbeat, we celebrate,
In this enchanted night, we contemplate.

Ethereal hues light our way,
Guiding us through the night's ballet.
With laughter and love, we celebrate,
In this winter wonder, it feels so great.

## Lanterns of Stars in a Crystal Sky

Beneath the twinkling gems above,
We dance in shadows, hearts aglow.
Each lantern whispers tales of love,
In a tapestry of light, we flow.

Children laughing, voices soar,
As laughter rings through every street.
With every step, we crave for more,
In this festival, life feels sweet.

Colors paint the canvas bright,
Pulsing beats, a joyful cheer.
We hold each other tight tonight,
With dreams to chase, and none to fear.

So let the stars guide us on high,
In the night's embrace, we thrive.
As lanterns dance in crystal sky,
Together, we come alive.

## Frosty Threads of Time

Amidst the frosty air so crisp,
We gather close, hand in hand.
With every breath, a jeweled wisp,
As time weaves stories, bold and grand.

The laughter echoes, merry and light,
In a world wrapped in winter's grace.
With each shared glance, hearts unite,
Creating magic in this place.

Snowflakes dance like tiny dreams,
Settling softly on our cheeks.
In the glow of the evening beams,
We cherish warmth and joy that peaks.

So let the frosty threads entwine,
In the tapestry of festive cheer.
In moments fleeting, we align,
For memories are what we hold dear.

## Nightfall's Peaceful Veil

As the sun dips low, the stars awake,
A gentle hush blankets the land.
With each heartbeat, the night we take,
Wrapped in dreams, united we stand.

Candles flicker, casting soft light,
Where shadows play a soothing song.
In tranquil moments, hearts take flight,
In this peaceful night, we belong.

Whispers of comfort in the breeze,
As night unfurls its starry quilt.
With every sigh, our worries cease,
In the calm, our spirits are built.

So let nightfall's veil surround,
A cocoon of love and peace so bright.
In this sacred space, joy is found,
As the world rests in the gentle night.

## Glacial Serenade of the Heart

In the hush of winter's breath,
A serenade begins to rise.
With melodies that dance like swath,
Whispers of warmth beneath the skies.

Each glacial note, a crystal sound,
Painting portraits in the air.
As harmony and laughter blend,
Together, we create and share.

The candles flicker, shadows play,
As joy cascades like falling snow.
In this festive night, we sway,
Hearts entwined, as passions glow.

So let the serenade be heard,
In the cadence of the night’s embrace.
With every heartbeat, love’s sweet word,
In this moment, we find our place.

## Crystal Dreams of Forgotten Warmth

In the glow of lanterns bright,
Laughter dances in the night.
Glasses raised with cheerful cheer,
Memories spark, as loved ones near.

Shimmering lights in every hue,
Hearts unite like morning dew.
Songs of joy fill the air,
Embraced by love, a moment rare.

Whispers of dreams in the frost,
Every smile cherished, not lost.
Under the stars, we craft our lore,
In warmth and laughter, we soar more.

Together we weave a tapestry bright,
Crystal dreams in the soft moonlight.
Bound by the magic of this embrace,
We'll remember this festive place.

## A Veil of Snow Over Sleep

A blanket white on slumbering earth,
Glistening softly, a winter's mirth.
Snowflakes twirl in playful dreams,
Joyful whispers, in silent streams.

Footprints trace where children play,
Building snowmen, bright and gay.
With hats and scarves of colors bold,
Each moment a treasure to hold.

Candles flicker, warmth inside,
Mugs of cocoa, friends beside.
Stories shared by the fireside glow,
A festive cheer that steals the show.

Wrapped in the magic of this night,
Softly shining, a pure delight.
In the embrace of winter’s keep,
A veil of snow over gentle sleep.

## Beneath the Starry Chill

Under a sky of twinkling stars,
Laughter rings from near and far.
Friends and family gather here,
In the crisp air, we share our cheer.

Fires crackle, their warmth surrounds,
A canvas of joy on this ground.
Music floats on the evening breeze,
Melodies sweet as the rustling trees.

Frosty breath in the chilly air,
A moment of magic for us to share.
Under the moon’s enchanting glow,
The festive spirit starts to flow.

With every laugh, our hearts align,
In the stillness, all feels divine.
Beneath the stars, our souls ignite,
Together we shine, a dazzling sight.

## Echoes of Sunlight in Ice

Reflections of joy in the winter's hold,
Echoes of sunlight, warm and bold.
Icicles glisten, a stunning display,
Nature's art in the festive array.

Families gather, smiles abound,
In the chill, warmth can be found.
Stories told by the fire's glow,
In our hearts, the warmth will grow.

With each cheer and each clasped hand,
We weave a bond, forever grand.
Through laughter's echo and joy's embrace,
Sunlight mingles in this place.

Memories crafted with love and light,
In the depth of winter, a glowing sight.
Echoes of sunlight in every heart,
A festival of warmth that won’t depart.

## Solstice Dreams in Crystal Light

In the heart of winter's glee,
Twinkling stars like gems set free,
Candles flicker, warm and bright,
A dance of dreams in crystal light.

Carols floating on the breeze,
Joy and laughter, hearts at ease,
Each moment shines with pure delight,
Wrapped within this cozy night.

Whispers of the season’s cheer,
Gathered loved ones ever near,
Sparkling eyes and smiles ignite,
We weave our dreams in crystal light.

With the fire's gentle glow,
Wishing well for those we know,
Hand in hand, we share this rite,
In the warmth of crystal light.

## Echoes of the Silent Night

Beneath the stars, the world holds still,
Softly rests on winter's chill,
Echoes dance in twinkling air,
Magic weaves through quiet care.

Snowflakes whisper as they fall,
Nature's hush, a sacred call,
Moonlight casts its silver glow,
In this night, our spirits grow.

Hearts are full, with peace we sigh,
As dreams of hope begin to fly,
Underneath the endless height,
Feel the warmth of silent night.

Hands entwined, we stand as one,
Blessed by all the love we've spun,
In sweet harmony, pure and bright,
We find our joy in silent night.

## Chilling Embrace of Longest Darkness

The night stretches, shadows sway,
Cold winds play and softly say,
Wrapped in blankets, snug and tight,
We find warmth in darkest night.

Frosted windows tell their tale,
Of winter's breath on every trail,
Stars are hidden, quiet and meek,
Yet in our hearts, a fire speaks.

Gathered close in cozy rooms,
Echoes chase away the glooms,
Together in this fleeting light,
Joyful warmth hugs longest night.

With each laugh, the cold recedes,
In friendship's warmth, our spirit feeds,
Together, hope takes glorious flight,
As we embrace the longest night.

## Frost-kissed Moments at Dawn

A shiver dances on the air,
Morning light begins to share,
Frost-kissed petals shimmer bright,
Whispers flourish in the light.

With every breath, a sparkle glows,
Nature wakes, as silence flows,
Golden rays break through the gray,
Chasing shadows far away.

Birds rejoice, their songs take flight,
Joyful sounds of pure delight,
Each moment, fresh and reborn,
Frost-kissed magic fills the morn.

As the world begins to wake,
We embrace what dreams may make,
In the warmth of sun's first light,
We find our joy in frosty sights.

## Chilling Echoes of Solitary Whispers

In the night when laughter flies,
Firelight dances, spirits rise.
Chilled winds carry tales of cheer,
Echoes of joy, we hold so dear.

Snowflakes twirl in moonlit skies,
Whispers soft as lullabies.
Hot cocoa warms our festive hearts,
Togetherness, where love imparts.

Candles flicker, shadows sway,
Memories crafted day by day.
In the glow, friendships gleam,
A tapestry of shared dreams.

As the stars begin to gleam,
We find our place, a joyous theme.
Chilling echoes, sweet and bright,
In this festive, winter night.

## Gardens Enshrouded in Frozen Time

In gardens where the frost does play,
Colors burst in shades of gray.
Twinkling lights like fireflies,
Beneath a canvas of twilight skies.

Laughter weaves through branches bare,
Whispers dance in wintry air.
Each step crunches with delight,
As joy blooms in serene white.

Gathered near the evergreen,
Stories shared beneath the sheen.
We celebrate the warmth within,
As hearts together rise and spin.

In this realm where time stands still,
Magic flows against our will.
Frozen gardens, memories sweet,
In our hearts, the season's beat.

## Winter's Veil: A Shimmering Tale

Winter wraps the world in dreams,
Sparkling white, or so it seems.
Stories shared by candlelight,
Laughter echoes through the night.

Snowmen stand with hats askew,
Children’s joy in every view.
Ribbons bright and colors warm,
Together we create a charm.

Fireplaces crackling loud,
Gathered close, a loving crowd.
In this glow, our hearts unite,
A dazzling feast on winter's night.

Through the veil of swirling snow,
Magic whispers, gentle flow.
A shimmering tale unfolds with grace,
In our hearts, each special place.

**Beneath the Hushed Vault of Stars**

Beneath the sky, so vast and wide,
We gather close, with hearts full of pride.
Stars like dreams in dark embrace,
A festive glow on every face.

The hush of night, a comforting shroud,
Wrapping us close in laughter loud.
S'mores and stories shared around,
In this moment, love is found.

Twirling lights on trees aglow,
Spirits lift where the soft winds blow.
Each flicker tells of joy and cheer,
Together we find a home right here.

Underneath this endless expanse,
We take a breath, embrace the chance.
Beneath the stars, our hearts entwine,
In festive wonder, we brightly shine.

## Whispers of Winter's Embrace

Snowflakes dance in gentle flight,
The world wrapped in silver light.
Children laugh, their hearts aglow,
In winter's grasp, our spirits flow.

Fireplaces crackle, warmth inside,
Cozy moments we can't hide.
Mugs of cocoa, marshmallows piled,
Joyful scenes, like dreams compiled.

Stars twinkle in the frosty sky,
As carolers sing, and time slips by.
Hugs and laughter fill the air,
In every minute, love we share.

With every chill, a warmth we find,
In winter's hug, our hearts entwined.
As evening falls, the world turns bright,
In whispers soft, we greet the night.

## Chilling Light at Dusk

The sun dips low, the sky ablaze,
In hues of orange, gold displays.
Crisp air carries a joyful tune,
As twilight falls, we dance to boon.

Candles flicker in the crisp air,
Families gather, hearts laid bare.
Laughter echoes down the street,
As night descends, we feel complete.

Frosted windows glisten bright,
Reflecting back the warm delight.
Winter's magic fills the space,
In chilling light, we find our grace.

With every smile, the warmth returns,
In moments shared, our spirit learns.
So let us raise a glass tonight,
To chilling light and love's pure light.

## Solstice Shadows on Ice

Underneath the silver moon,
We skate together, hearts in tune.
Solstice shadows whisk us away,
In swirling patterns, we softly sway.

Frosted breath on rosy cheeks,
In joyful laughter, the moment peaks.
Songs of the season fill the night,
As we glide on in pure delight.

Candles flicker, casting glow,
With every turn, the magic flows.
Together we weave a tapestry,
Of joyful moments, wild and free.

As dawn breaks on this winter day,
The shadows dance as children play.
In icy realms, our bonds will stay,
Solstice whispers guide our way.

## Frigid Dreams in a Crystal Landscape

In a world of white, so vast and bright,
Dreams take flight in the sparkling light.
Snow-covered trees, a wondrous sight,
A crystal landscape, pure delight.

The silence deep, a peaceful song,
As nature's magic pulls us along.
With every snowflake, a tale is spun,
In frigid dreams, our hearts are one.

Icicles shimmering from rooftops high,
Like diamonds frozen, they catch the eye.
Children frolic, their glee unbound,
In this winter realm, joy is found.

So let us wander, hand in hand,
Through this enchanting winter land.
With laughter and love, our spirits soar,
In frigid dreams, forevermore.

## Frosted apparitions of Quietude

Whispers of snowflakes drift and twirl,
Laughter echoes in a soft, warm swirl.
Children's gleeful voices rise and play,
As frost-kissed dreams dance the night away.

Candles flicker in the winter's glow,
Warmth and joy in each heart they sow.
Mornings wrapped in blankets, pure and bright,
Frosted apparitions greet the light.

Glistening paths weave through the trees,
A tapestry formed by the icy breeze.
Amidst the hush, the world seems to pause,
In moments of peace, love gently draws.

Starlit skies blanket the evening's glee,
A celebration of all we can be.
Joined together in this festive cheer,
Frosted apparitions whisper near.

## Ephemeral Glories in Icy Hues

Beneath the moon’s soft, silvery glance,
The world is dressed for a joyous dance.
Icicles shimmer with a radiant light,
Ephemeral glories ignite the night.

Laughter rings out in the crisp, cold air,
As families gather, love everywhere.
In shimmering coats, we twirl and spin,
Embracing the magic that lies within.

Sparkling snowflakes like diamonds fall,
Each flurry whispers a festive call.
Children chase dreams in a winter's embrace,
Moments of joy in this enchanted space.

With hearts aglow, we cherish the time,
Creating together a rhythm, a rhyme.
Ephemeral glories, bright as the stars,
Reflect our joys in this life that is ours.

## Chills of a Starry Night

Under the blanket of a starry sky,
Laughter and stories begin to fly.
Chills of night dance with warmth of cheer,
As hearts come together, holding dear.

Snowflakes shimmer on each frozen branch,
A soft glow invites us to take a chance.
Warm cups of cocoa, hugs wrapped so tight,
Fill the cold air with sweet delight.

Dreams take flight on this frosty eve,
A tapestry woven, we silently weave.
Chills of the night yet tenderly warm,
Nature’s embrace, a comforting charm.

In the quiet, we hear the laughter’s ring,
As bells of joy through the silence sing.
Chills of a starry night weave the threads,
Of memories cherished, where love gently spreads.

## A Dance of Light in the Dark

As dusk falls softly, the stars align,
A dance of light starts to intertwine.
With every twinkle, the world ignites,
Hope unfurls in the cold, crisp nights.

Lanterns aglow on the paths we tread,
A sparkling pathway where dreams are fed.
Joyful hearts beat in a rhythmic flow,
As darkness retreats, new wonders grow.

Fires crackle with a comforting song,
Uniting us all in a harmony strong.
Together we blossom, together we play,
A dance of light, come what may.

The night is alive with laughter and cheer,
In this festive space, we hold each dear.
A dance of light illuminates the dark,
In each glowing moment, we leave our mark.

## Timeless Glimmer Beneath the Snow

Beneath the blanket, soft and white,
Laughter dances, hearts feel light.
Twinkling stars in frosty air,
Joyful whispers everywhere.

Children sledding, spirits soar,
Nature's hush, we all explore.
Crafting dreams in purest snow,
Moments cherished, time moves slow.

Bonfires crackle, stories shared,
Warmth of friendship shows we cared.
As embers glow and laughter rings,
In this magic, our hearts take wings.

Every glance, a twinkling gaze,
Captured in this winter haze.
Timeless glimmer, pure delight,
Beneath the snow, we find our light.

## Reflections in a Frosted Mirror

Frosted panes with tales to tell,
Snowflakes whisper, all is well.
Glistening paths where shadows play,
In the stillness, hearts will sway.

Candles flicker, warm and bright,
Guiding us through winter's night.
Reflections dance with golden hue,
Memories cherished, fresh and new.

Joyful gatherings, spirits high,
Festive bells ring in the sky.
In this moment, all we seek,
Love and laughter, rich and sweet.

As we toast to times gone by,
With every spark, we reach the sky.
Frosted mirrors show our grace,
In this season, we find our place.

## Twilight's Breath on Frozen Ground

Twilight settles, colors blend,
Whispers soft, as day will end.
Frozen ground in twilight's glow,
Magic dances, spirits flow.

Crisp air carries sweet delight,
Twinkling lights adorn the night.
Gathered close, we share our dreams,
In this warmth, love gently beams.

Echoes of laughter fill the air,
Moments woven, treasures rare.
Under stars that brightly gleam,
Hearts unite, as time will dream.

Songs of joy on winter's breath,
Celebrating life, not death.
On frozen ground, our souls ignite,
In twilight's breath, we feel the light.

## Shimmering Silence of Stillness

In the stillness, peace unfolds,
Shimmering silence, secrets told.
Every flake, a whispered prayer,
Echoes soft, float in the air.

Moonlight casts its gentle glow,
Illuminating paths of snow.
In each step, a quiet grace,
Nature's rhythm, a warm embrace.

Twinkling stars, a cosmic dance,
Inviting us to take a chance.
Celebrate this magic found,
In the shimmering, soft surround.

Hearts rejoicing, spirits free,
In this silence, we just be.
Timeless moments, pure and bright,
Shimmering stillness, pure delight.

## When Night Stretches Long

The stars are twinkling high above,
Moonlight dances on the trees.
Laughter bubbles like a stream,
Joy ignites the winter's breeze.

Friends gather 'round the fire bright,
Sharing stories, warm embrace.
A tapestry of pure delight,
Glowing hearts, a sacred space.

With each note of melody,
Voices rise like silver streams.
In this night, sweet harmony,
Fulfilling all our brightest dreams.

As shadows play, and sparks take flight,
We toast to love and memories.
When night stretches long, purest light,
Forever held, our spirits free.

## The Coldest Breath of Longing

In the silence, snowflakes fall,
Whispers echo through the night.
A chill wraps around us all,
Yet hearts are warm with pure delight.

Glowing candles flicker bright,
Casting warmth upon the wall.
Gathered close in festive light,
We find joy within it all.

Each smile shared, a spark ignites,
Stories painted in the air.
Through the coldest winter nights,
Together we obliterate despair.

Beneath the frost, the fire glows,
In every laugh, a melody.
In the coldest breath, love shows,
A festive heart, in harmony.

## In the Heart of Winter's Grasp

Icicles hang like crystal tears,
Nature sleeps, yet we arise.
Around us, laughter, joy appears,
A festive spirit in our eyes.

Fires crackle, warmth enclosed,
We dance and spin, feet entwined.
Storytellers, each one posed,
With magic tales we've often mined.

In this heart of winter's grasp,
Hope flourishes, bright and clear.
Fingers clasped in perfect clasp,
Love surrounds us, drawing near.

As the world fades into white,
We celebrate, in pure delight.
In the snow, our dreams take flight,
In unison, hearts unite.

## Eclipsed by the Moon's Shimmer

Beneath the moon, a silver glow,
The night adorned in sparkles bright.
Each soul dances, lost in flow,
Eclipsed by the moon's shimmering light.

Voices weave a pastel song,
Each note floating on the breeze.
Together, we can't go wrong,
With love reflected in the trees.

Moments cherished, fleeting now,
Yet in these dreams, we stay alive.
With every whisper, we avow,
The festive spirit will survive.

North winds sing, and joy explodes,
Gathered hearts, united throng.
In the stillness, we've composed,
A tapestry where we belong.

## Dance of the Frigid Winds

Whispers in the frosty air,
The night is bright, no need to care.
Laughter echoes, spirits rise,
Beneath a canvas of starry skies.

Snowflakes twirl like dancers fair,
Each glimmer catches dreams to share.
Children's joy, a pure delight,
As they play in the sparkling light.

Hot cocoa sipped by fireside glow,
Stories unfold, their warmth to show.
Frosty branches, a silver crown,
In this wonderland, hearts won't frown.

Together we'll make memories last,
Setting footfalls in winter's past.
Embracing the chill, our spirits soar,
In the dance of the cold we adore.

## Celestial Frost's Gentle Caress

Under the moon's soft, glowing beam,
Winter weaves its frosty dream.
Each breath a cloud that drifts away,
In this magical, snowy ballet.

Icicles hang like diamonds bright,
Reflecting hues of silver light.
Nature's blanket, pure and white,
Transforming the earth into pure delight.

Crisp laughter rings through frozen air,
In holiday cheer, we find our share.
Holding hands, we weave through snow,
In a world where love can grow.

Beneath the stars, calm and serene,
We dance through the night, a beautiful scene.
In the chill, we find our grace,
Embraced by winter's loving embrace.

## Winter's Touch on Slumbering Earth

The world wraps tight in winter's fold,
Silent nights, stories untold.
The trees stand tall with coats of white,
Cradling dreams in the stillness of night.

Blankets of snow on rooftops lie,
Reflecting warmth in the starlit sky.
Each flake a whisper, crisp and clear,
Calling us close to those we hold dear.

Fires crackle with lively cheer,
As memories gather, drawing near.
Mirthful songs fill the chilled air,
Celebrating life, beyond despair.

In winter's arms, happiness beams,
Wrapped in love, we live our dreams.
Together we stand, hearts entwined,
In this enchanted season, joy aligned.

## Enchanted in a Shroud of Ice

Amidst the frost, a hush prevails,
Nature dons her frosty veils.
Glimmering trees, a sight divine,
In the cold, all souls entwine.

With each step, the crunching sound,
Echoes of laughter all around.
Playful snowballs, a spirited fight,
In this enchanted world, hearts take flight.

With every swirl, the magic grows,
A tapestry woven as winter flows.
Friends and family gather near,
In this frosty realm, spreading cheer.

Glistening paths lead us to explore,
As music of joy begins to soar.
Under the stars, our spirits free,
In this shroud of ice, we dance with glee.

## Ethereal Magic of a Winter's Night

Stars sparkle bright in the dark blue sky,
Snowflakes dance gently as they drift by.
Candles aglow in windows they gleam,
Whispers of wonder, a soft, tender dream.

Laughter and cheer fill the chilly air,
Voices like music, a joyful affair.
Families gather, their hearts closely knit,
Wrapped in the warmth of love, every bit.

The world's a canvas of white and of gold,
Stories of magic and warmth to be told.
Trees decked with lights, a shimmering sight,
In this winter eve, hearts feel so light.

Ethereal moments that linger and sway,
Breathless with joy, we embrace the play.
As night wraps its arms in a shimmering cloak,
We dance with the stars, as dreams softly evoke.

## Tranquil Whispers From the Frost's Heart

Moonlight weaves silver on fields laid to rest,
Softly it beckons, a retreat so blessed.
Chill in the air, yet warm is the glow,
Of fireside stories and love we bestow.

A blanket of silence, the world slows its pace,
In the stillness we find our own special space.
Candlelight flickers, its glow so divine,
Whispers of winter, a peace that will shine.

Each breath is a mist, painting air with our hopes,
Laughter like echoes, like sweet, playful ropes.
Through frosty landscapes our hearts dance with grace,
Tranquil connections in this sacred place.

Stars glimmer gently, holding secrets untold,
Embraced by the night, wrapped in stories old.
Each moment we cherish, a gift pure and rare,
In the frost's gentle heart, we find love, laid bare.

## A Serenade for the Winter Moon

Under a blanket of twinkling delight,
Carols are sung in the magical night.
With each gentle note, spirits take flight,
A serenade forming in pure moonlight.

Sleigh bells are ringing, a sweet, merry sound,
Echoes of joy in the warmth all around.
Candles are flickering, casting their glow,
As shadows are dancing on newly laid snow.

Gathered together, we share laughter and cheer,
Moments of magic that bring us all near.
A tapestry woven with love and delight,
Each thread a memory, holding on tight.

The winter moon smiles, a guardian so bright,
Showering magic in the heart of the night.
In this festive season, our souls intertwine,
A serenade echoes, forever divine.

## Journey Through a Winter Dreamscape

Snowflakes dance under the moon,
Sparkling like gems in the night.
Children laugh with joy and glee,
As stars twinkle, shining bright.

Lanterns glow on frosted trees,
Whispers of magic fill the air.
Footprints lead through drifts of white,
Creating paths without a care.

Cocoa warms our chilly hands,
While carolers sing in the square.
The world transformed in winter's grasp,
A dreamscape soft and rare.

Together we embrace the chill,
In this season so divine.
With every laugh and every cheer,
We weave our hearts, intertwine.

## Fables of Ice in the Midnight Air

Glittering tales unfold tonight,
Underneath the starlit skies.
Ice castles gleam, a wondrous sight,
Where magic breathes and never dies.

The world wrapped in a silken sheet,
Of frost that glimmers, soft and bright.
Whispers of fables in the street,
Carried on the winds of night.

Fairy lights dance along the way,
As laughter echoes through the dark.
With each heart a joyful spray,
Creating warmth, igniting spark.

In every corner, stories grow,
Of winter wonder, pure delight.
In this season, we flow,
Fables of ice that feel just right.

## Reverie of a Winter's Star

Beneath the hush of winter's breath,
A star shines brightly from above.
Its light a beacon, guiding souls,
In the chill that wraps us, gentle love.

We wander through this snowy maze,
With dreams alight in every heart.
The night adorned with silver lace,
In this moment, we shall never part.

Candles flicker in the dark,
Casting shadows on frozen ground.
With every whisper, every spark,
Magic lingers all around.

So let us dance beneath the glow,
Of winter's dream, our spirits soar.
In reverie, we share the show,
Together, forever, we will explore.

## Radiance in a Shattered Frost

As morning breaks on icy land,
A canvas painted bright and bold.
Crystals fracture, each a gem,
In radiance, stories unfold.

The sun arises, melting dreams,
Transforming frost to sparkling dew.
With every beam, a new path gleams,
Awakening life, fresh and new.

Children run, their laughter rings,
As cheer fills the spaces once cold.
In this moment, pure joy springs,
We gather warmth, a sight to behold.

Together we share in the light,
In a world that glimmers with grace.
With hearts aglow, we take flight,
Creating memories we embrace.

## Crystal Whispers in the Wind

Glistening flakes dance high,
Under moonlight's soft sigh.
Joyful laughter fills the air,
Hearts alight without a care.

Children's eyes gleam so bright,
Chasing dreams in the night.
Every step makes a sound,
Magic twirls all around.

Friends gather by the fire,
Offering warmth and desire.
Toasting marshmallows with glee,
Sharing stories, wild and free.

As the stars twinkle clear,
Love and laughter draw near.
In this moment, we find bliss,
Wrapped in winter’s pure kiss.

## Haiku of a Frosted Breeze

Gentle breezes flow,
Snowflakes twirl in the moonlight,
Winter's breath whispers.

Trees wear silver crowns,
Nature's beauty shines so bright,
Stillness wraps the night.

Crisp air, laughter rings,
Celebrations fill the heart,
Life in every breath.

Frosted dreams take flight,
Underneath the sparkling sky,
Joy in every glance.

## Veins of Ice Beneath the Surface

Crimson and gold aglow,
Ice veins whisper below.
Nature's canvas unfolds,
Silent stories to be told.

Beneath winter's embrace,
Seasons dance with quiet grace.
Magic pulses from deep,
In the night, secrets keep.

Joyful hearts gather tight,
As flames flicker with light.
In the warmth, fingers entwined,
Memories sweetly designed.

With each laugh, we shine,
Through the chill, love entwines.
Under the icy veil,
Unity will prevail.

## Winter's Lullaby in the Moonlight

Softly, snowflakes fall,
Wrapping the world in a shawl.
Moonlight sings a sweet song,
Guiding us where we belong.

Whispers of dreams ignite,
Each moment feels just right.
Children's giggles fill the air,
Wonder blooms everywhere.

Families gather near,
Sharing tales, spreading cheer.
Gentle warmth, hearts awake,
In this magic, we partake.

As night deepens its hold,
Memories, precious as gold.
In winter's gentle embrace,
We find peace in this place.

## Silenced Footprints in Powdered White

In the hush of falling snow,
Children dance, laughter aglow.
A blanket soft, so pure and bright,
Covers all in gleeful light.

Whispers of joy fill the air,
As snowflakes twirl without a care.
Footprints fade, no trace to find,
Magic lingers, hearts aligned.

Warmth in mugs, and cheeks aglow,
Wondrous visions start to grow.
Cherished moments round the fire,
As dreams and hopes lift ever higher.

Beneath the stars, we gather near,
Sharing songs, spreading cheer.
In this world of white delight,
Every soul shines through the night.

## The Essence of Crystal Clarity

Glistening gems on branches sway,
Nature's art in bright array.
Crystal droplets catch the light,
Transforming day to pure delight.

Beneath the sun, they dance and gleam,
Each a part of winter's dream.
Brisk air filled with laughter's cheer,
Echoes of joy, all gathered here.

Children's voices fill the scene,
Building laughter, crisp and keen.
Snowmen rise with hats askew,
In festive spirit, the world feels new.

Evenings close with fireside warmth,
Sharing stories, hearts take form.
In this realm of sparkling shine,
Every soul is intertwined.

## Veil of Frost on Moonlit Waters

A shimmering sheen on silent lakes,
Frosty whispers where magic wakes.
Moonlight drapes a silver veil,
Guiding dreams through winter's tale.

Reflections twinkling, stars above,
Nature's canvas, a gift of love.
Cold winds hum a soothing tune,
As night wraps all in brightened gloom.

Each breath a cloud that fans the night,
In the stillness, hearts unite.
Together we watch the world unfold,
As stories of old in silence, told.

The frost, a cloak of beauty spun,
In this moment, we are one.
In moonlit grace, we find our way,
On the waters where spirits play.

## Luminous Solitude in Winter's Grasp

A solitary path of white,
Cradled gently by the night.
In the quiet, peace abounds,
Footsteps soft on frozen grounds.

Stars like diamonds twinkle bright,
Guiding souls with silver light.
Winter's breath, crisp and clear,
Wraps around us, drawing near.

Moments stolen, time stands still,
In the beauty, hearts are filled.
Whispers shared beneath the sky,
Luminous dreams that seem to fly.

In solitude we find a spark,
A secret joy that lights the dark.
Through winter's chill, we stand, we sway,
Bound by warmth, in frost we play.

www.ingramcontent.com/pod-product-compliance
Ingram Content Group UK Ltd.
Pitfield, Milton Keynes, MK11 3LW, UK
UKHW030846221224
452712UK00006B/484

9 789908 117508